TAKE A WALK
ON THE
WILD SIDE

KATYA'S BUSY MORNING

BY THEA FELDMAN

Animal Planet

© 2006 Discovery Communications, Inc.
Animal Planet and logo are trademarks
of Discovery Communications, Inc.,
used under license. All rights reserved.
www.animalplanet.com

Design by E. Friedman
Contributing consultant Dr. Robert W. Shumaker
of the Great Ape Trust of Iowa

© 2006 by Meredith Corporation.
First Edition. Printed in the USA, bound in Mexico.
All rights reserved.
ISBN: 0-696-23292-8
Meredith Books
Des Moines, Iowa

It was a warm spring morning in the forest. Katya was awake early and slipped away before her cubs woke up. Katya was hungry. She hoped to find food to feed her three hungry sons, Ivan, Oleg, and Yakov.

GRRR-reat to Know!

Tigers are the biggest cats in the world. They can be 10 feet long and weigh up to 600 pounds.

The morning was passing quickly and Katya had not found anything to eat yet. She decided it was time to head back to her cubs. As she crossed the meadow she saw something move and went to investigate.

GRRR-reat to Know!
Tigers are the only wild cats with stripes, and no two tigers have the same pattern of stripes. In fact, that's how scientists tell tigers apart.

Slowly and silently Katya moved through the tall grass and into a stand of trees. Was something in there? Did she hear something? What might it be? Katya was getting hungrier and hungrier.

GRRR-reat to Know!

An adult tiger needs its own territory that includes a forested area with plenty of food and water. The size of the territory depends on the availability of food and can range from 40 to 400 square miles.

Suddenly Katya heard the sound of rustling leaves and grass. Something was there! She could feel its movement beneath her paws. Katya took a deep sniff through her open mouth to see if she could tell what it was.

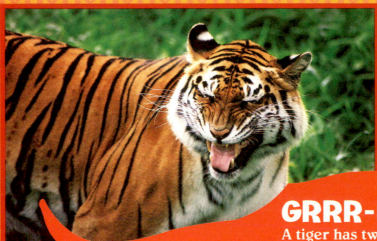

GRRR-reat to Know!

A tiger has two tiny openings in the roof of its mouth that increases its sense of smell and ability to detect odors.

Ever so slowly and silently, Katya poked her head through the underbrush and she saw . . . nothing! Whatever had been there disappeared. She stood very still while she tried to figure out where her breakfast might have gone.

GRRR-reat to Know!
Tigers are hunters and must search for their food, so they are always alert to different sights and sounds.

Over there! Katya saw a burst of movement on the other side of the brush. She sprang into action ready to catch a tasty meal.

GRRR-reat to Know!

Tigers often leap when they are on a hunt. Tigers can leap more than 30 feet! They can also run—for short bursts—at speeds of 35 miles an hour.

As Katya jumped over the brush she saw water on the other side. It was too late to stop. What a surprise Katya had when she landed with a big splash!

GRRR-reat to Know!

Tigers are very good swimmers. They can swim up to distances of 18 miles with ease!

GRRR-reat to Know!

Tigers are one of the few kinds of cats that like water. Water keeps them cool in very hot weather.

Katya felt refreshed by the cool water, but she was still hungry. Water dripped from her fur and whiskers as she headed back to wake her cubs. Breakfast for Katya would have to wait.

Right now Katya had more important things to do . . . like feed her cubs. Katya returned to her den, making sure that no predators saw where her cubs were. She picked up the cubs, one by one, with her teeth and brought them out into the warm morning sun.

GRRR-reat to Know!

Most tigers have yellow eyes. Tigers rely mostly on eyesight when hunting. During the day their eyesight is about as good as yours. But at night, it's much better!

First, Katya gave each of her cubs a bath with her tongue. Katya knew how important it was to keep them clean. She did not want a predator to pick up their scent. If a predator found the den while she was out hunting she would be unable to protect her little ones.

GRRR-reat to Know!

A tiger cub is born blind and helpless, weighing a little over two pounds. Tiger cubs don't hunt on their own until they are two years old.

When the cubs began to cry, Katya knew that while her breakfast could wait, her cubs needed to eat now. She laid down on the soft grass and nursed Ivan, Oleg, and Yakov.

GRRR-reat to Know!
When cubs are six months old, they accompany their mother on searches for food, often practicing by jumping on her tail.

Katya knew she could find food for herself later. Her cubs were safe and happy, and their tummies were full. Ivan, Oleg, and Yakov were ready for a day of romping, wrestling, and learning, and that was the most important thing to Katya.